THE VICTORIA AND ALBERT COLOUR BOOKS

LIBRARY OF CONGRESS CATALOG CARD NO: 87-73342

ISBN 0-8109-1739-4

COPYRIGHT © WEBB & BOWER (PUBLISHERS) LIMITED, EXETER,
THE TRUSTEES OF THE VICTORIA AND ALBERT MUSEUM, LONDON,
CARROLL, DEMPSEY & THIRKELL LIMITED 1988

BOOK, COVER AND SLIPCASE DESIGN BY CARROLL, DEMPSEY & THIRKELL LIMITED

PUBLISHED IN 1988 BY HARRY N. ABRAMS, INCORPORATED, NEW YORK
ALL RIGHTS RESERVED. NO PART OF THE CONTENTS OF THIS BOOK MAY BE
REPRODUCED WITHOUT THE WRITTEN PERMISSION OF THE PUBLISHER

A TIMES MIRROR COMPANY

TYPESET BY OPTIC

PRINTED AND BOUND IN HONG KONG

THE VICTORIA AND ALBERT COLOUR BOOKS

DESIGNS FOR SHAWLS

INTRODUCTION BY
HILARY YOUNG

HARRY N. ABRAMS, INC., PUBLISHERS
NEW YORK

THE DESIGN for shawl fabrics reproduced here are the work of an Englishman, George Haité (1825-71). Like most of his contemporaries in the textile designing trades Haité is today an elusive and shadowy figure. The reasons for this are not hard to identify, for the majority of early and mid-Victorian designers 'were unknown and it was the custom and object of manufacturers to keep their names secret.'

That George Haité is remembered today is largely because of the efforts of his son George Charles Haité (1855-1924), himself a prolific pattern designer. He preserved a large number of his father's designs and presented sixty of them to the Victoria and Albert Museum in 1911. Earlier, in 1897, he had reproduced three of them in the first of two rambling articles, *On the Design and Designers of the Victorian Reign*, that he contributed to the *Architectural Review*. These articles, from which the above quotation is taken, contain a few tantalizing references to his father's work; and by drawing on these, and on the census returns for the designer's family, it has been possible to piece together the following fragmentary account.

George Haité was born in late 1825 in the textile printing parish of Mitcham, which is situated on the River Wandle in Surrey. His father was a calico printer and his uncle, John Haité was a textile designer: a small packet of the latter's designs for printed cottons, elegantly inscribed *Spring Patterns for The Year. 1813,* is at this museum.

By putting together two of G.C. Haité's remarks – that his father was one of the leading pattern designers of the old school of the period of Queen Victoria's ascension, and that 'it was at Swaisland's that most, if not all, of the good old-fashioned designers matriculated in the good old-fashioned manner of apprenticeship' – one can infer that George Haité may have been apprenticed at Swaisland's printworks at Crayford in Kent. Of this there is no proof – and it has not proved possible to locate him in the Crayford census

returns – but his parents were certainly living in this parish in 1841, at which date Haité must have been about seventeen years of age.

Wherever he 'matriculated', a connection with Swaisland's can be proven for the year 1847, for a volume of their designs, now the property of the textile firm G. P. and J. Baker, has loose covers one of which is inscribed *G. Haité 1847.* This volume, some of the sheets in which are dated *1845*, provides the earliest documentary evidence for Haité's work as a designer of shawl patterns.

Although he must have spent the greater part of his adult life working for the Kent and Surrey printworks, when Haité married in 1853 both he and his wife gave an address in the Strand, London, where the couple must have had lodgings. His occupation was recorded as 'Designer', and his age as 27. Whether he was at that time working for the London textile industry is not known, but he was not at this address in 1851, and by about 1854 he was living in the parish of Bexley in Kent.

Haité remained in Bexley until about 1858-60. In July 1855, when G.C. Haité was born, the family gave an address in Bexley Heath. It is clear from the census returns of 1851 and 1861 that Bexley Heath's inhabitants included a large number of workers for the textile industries. Among those listed are several silk and calico printers, printblock cutters, and a number of designers. One of the designers was described as a 'Pattern Designer for Silks and Shawls', suggesting that others from the area were involved in the production of shawls and shawl-patterned fabrics of the type that Haité designed.

Bexley Heath was not itself situated on a river – a prerequisite for textile bleaching, dyeing and printing – and it is probable that many of these workers were employed a mile away at Crayford. As noted above Haité was supplying designs for production at Crayford in 1847, and he may have continued to do so during the following decade: in 1906 he was referred to as a 'former Crayford designer'.

By 1860 Haité had returned to Mitcham, where he seems to have remained for the rest of his life. Among his close neighbours at Mitcham was Peter Dempsey, the proprietor of the Ravensbury printworks, who was described in 1861 as a 'Shawl and Silk Printer'. In the same year there were at least three other shawl printers living nearby – Alfred Crawford, John Pratt and John Tully – and it seems likely that Haité would have had business connections with these men during the early 1860s. In any case Mitcham was located near to other textile printing villages and towns – Hackbridge, Beddington, Mordon, Merton and Garrett – where Haité may have found work as a freelance designer.

The 'Cashmere' patterns that Haité designed for the Kent and Surrey printworks are derived from those of woven woollen shawls made in the Indian province of Kashmir. The introduction of the shawl in Europe and its consequent effects on the Kashmir industry make up one of the most fascinating chapters in the history of Indo-European stylistic currents. The successive stages of this have been admirably set out by John Irwin in *Shawls* (1955), from which the following account is partly derived.

The basic unit of design of the earliest surviving Indian shawls is a slender flower, a motif of Persian derivation that became merged with another Indo-

Persian device, the vase-of-flowers. During the course of the 18th century this in turn became transformed into a highly conventionalized shape, known in Britain today as the Paisley 'pine' or 'cone' after the prevalence of this device on the shawls produced in the Scottish town of Paisley in the 19th century.

In his *Descriptive Sketch of Changes in the Style of Paisley Shawls*, William Cross described the 'pine' motif thus: 'What is called the Pine in Indian patterns, is not an imitation of the rich fruit known by that name, nor the kind of fir so called... Its general form is that of an elegantly proportioned vase, tapering off at the neck into a gracefully curved beak or proboscis. This form... soon became, and long continued, the leading feature in shawl patterns. [It] reigned so paramount over all other forms that, like the round hat, it was often complained of as too common,... It seemed to be as essential in shawl ornamentation as the pediment is in Greek, or the pointed arch, in Gothic architecture.'

William Cross's account was published in 1872, by which date the great European vogue for Kashmir shawls, and for their British and French imitations, was declining. The Indian shawl is first recorded being worn as an article of fashionable western dress during the third quarter of the 18th century, and in this the English were probably in advance of the French. Importation led to emulation, and manufacture of imitation Indian shawls was established at Norwich, Edinburgh and Paisley by the first quarter of the 19th century.

Weaving of 'Indian' shawls began later in France than it did in Britain, but by the mid-19th century 'Cashmere' shawl design was dominated by the work of French designers and merchants, both in western Europe and in India. Their agents intervened in the manufacture of genuine Kashmir shawls, encouraging Indian weavers to follow designs that were suited to the western export markets. This was not, however, a new development: a similar situation regarding the activities of British merchants had been noted in Kashmir by William Moorcroft, an Englishman, as early as 1822.

Just as the French came to wield considerable influence on the design of

DESIGNS FOR SHAWLS

shawls woven in Kashmir, so too did they on those produced in Britain. William Cross, writing of the Paisley shawls of the late 1830s, stated that 'the inundation of French taste, working on Eastern ideas, soon carried all before it. The hybrid patterns that so originated were often sufficiently grotesque, combining Turkish, Indian, and Chinese objects into a strange *melange* more extravagant than beautiful.' This dependence on French prototypes was probably equally prevalent in England: certainly Swaisland's printworks, for example, were obtaining French designs and printed patterns during the 1840s and 1850s.

Again according to Cross, by the 1840s the 'pine' or 'cone' of shawl design was 'no longer simply the graceful, swelling, gourd-like figure with proud arching neck and majestic head, laurelled or wreathed as formerly. It was bent and twisted in all directions and generally drawn in couples or groups of three, with heads facing differently, and their outlines intricately intertwined'.

Three large designs – measuring up to 125 cm and datable to the years around 1850 – illustrate well the 'strange *melange* more extravagant than beautiful', and the prevailing fashion for 'cones' bent and twisted in all directions' that Cross described *(plates 19 and 20 show details).* In one of these, a design comparable to those of shawls shown at the Great Exhibition of 1851, naturalistic flowers that are entirely western in style are shown blooming forth from the centre of the Indian 'cone'. These drawings are for deep shawl borders; in this they are exceptional among Haité's designs at the Museum, the majority being for smaller repeating patterns intended for shawl centres or for dress fabrics, or for narrow outer borders which are datable to the later 1850s and 1860s *(plates 23, 25, 27, 28)*.

The precise dating of Haité's designs awaits further research. Nevertheless it is clear that the drawings at the Victoria and Albert Museum must span the greater part, if not the whole, of his adult life. Since the drawings passed into his son's possession, it seems likely that Haité worked as a freelance designer for much of his career, and that these sheets were among those that remained unsold at the time of his death in 1871. A further 201 of his shawl designs were presented to the Paisley Museum by his granddaughter in 1957, although nothing has yet come to light that suggests that Haité ever worked for the Paisley industry or for other Scottish manufacturers. Together these two collections comprise 261 designs, which represents a substantial and presumably unremunerated outlay in effort, time, and ingenuity on the part of the designer.

According to his son's account Haité was not content with his position within the trade: so keen was his 'disgust' and 'disappointment' that he 'declared over and over again that nothing would persuade him to allow me [G. C. Haité] to follow design as a means of livelihood'. He recognized that designers were 'the slaves of the fashion of the hour, the style of the season, and the middleman ... who blew hot and cold as the market demanded'. Referring to one of his father's designs G. C. Haité commented that 'the same designer who created this cashmere pattern, which is absolutely a beautiful specimen of Design ..., was compelled to vitiate his taste and set his judgement in defiance' by executing other work as the market dictated, thus 'humbling, if not degrading, his Art'.

George Haité died of smallpox at Mitcham in July 1871. At 45 he was by no means old; but in one respect his death was not untimely. For by the early 1870s the printed shawl fabrics that he had designed were declining in the esteem of the fashionable world, and had he lived longer he would undoubtedly have been compelled to 'vitiate his taste' and 'degrade his Art' still further.

BIBLIOGRAPHY

J. T. Brown, 'Swaisland's Printworks', *Crayford Parish Magazine*, August 1906.

William Cross, *Descriptive Sketch of Changes in the Style of Paisley Shawls*, 1872.

G. C. Haité, 'On the Design and Designers of the Victorian Reign', *Architectural Review*, Vol. II, 1897, pp. 81-9 and 141-6.

John Irwin, *Shawls*, 1955.

Natalie Rothstein and Wendy Hefford, 'Shawls and Other Textiles: The Coming of Mechanisation to the Loom', *British Textile Design in The Victoria and Albert Museum* (Ed. Donald King), Volume III, pp. xxii-xxiii.

Victoria and Albert Museum, *From East to West: Textiles from G. P. & J.* Baker, exhibition catalogue, 1984, cat. 74, and pp. 28-30.

I am indebted to Wendy Hefford, E. N. Montague, Sally MacDonald and Valerie Reilly for their help in preparing this introduction.

Haité's designs are drawn in bodycolour and watercolour over preliminary pencil on tracing or cream wove paper. The largest of the three deep borders measures 125 x 41 cm, *(plates 19 and 20)* and the remaining designs range from 36.5 x 26.5 cm *(plate 12)* to 9.7 x 6.3 cm *(plate 22, bottom right)*. The accession numbers for the group are E.4410-E.4469-1911.

THE PLATES

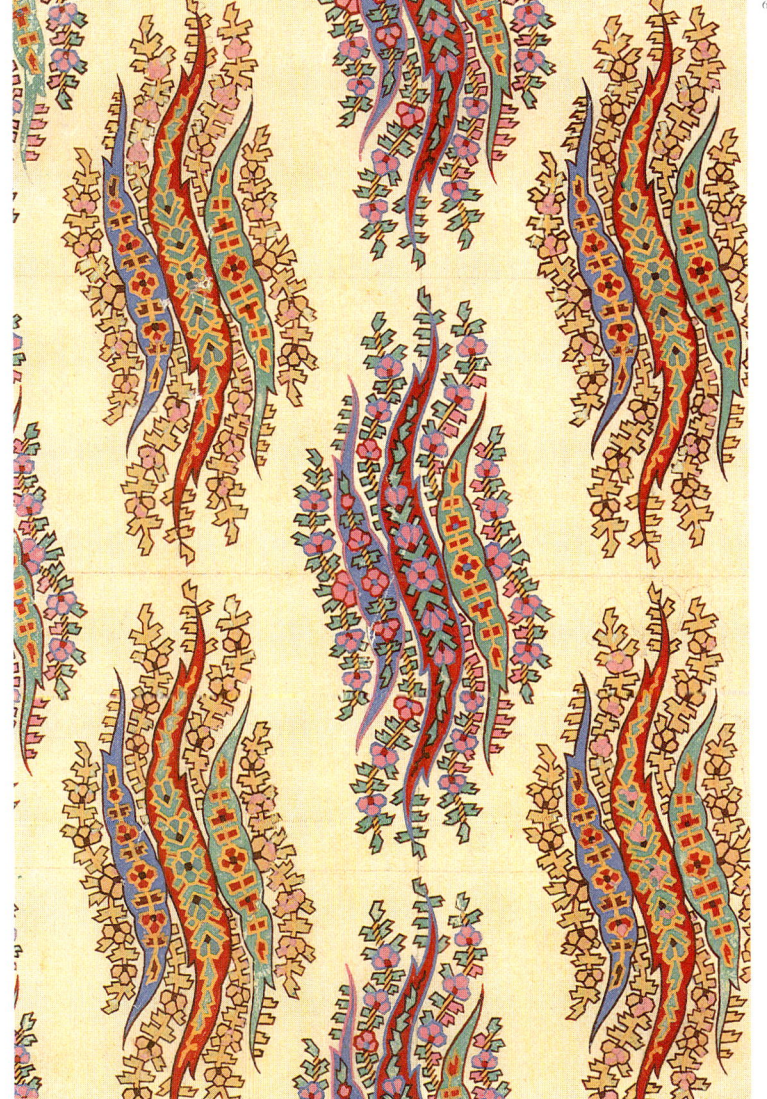

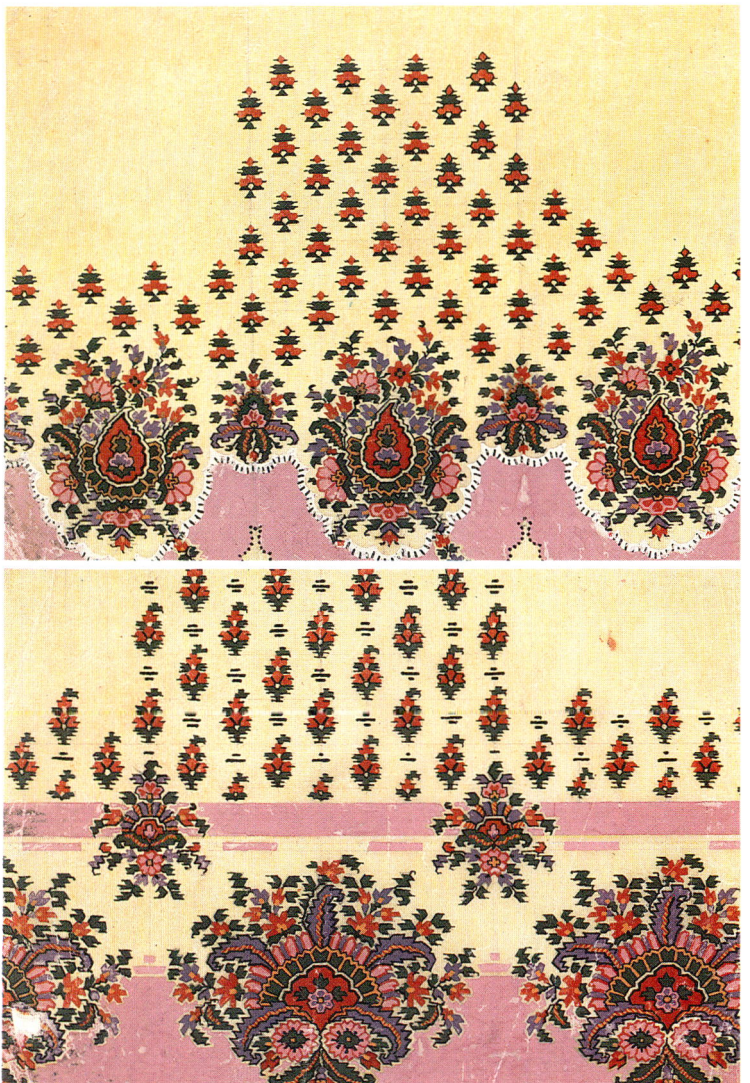

25

29